3 6501 00512153 3

REGION OF WAT

AT THE GATES OF THE THEME PARK

AT THE GATES OF THE THEME PARK

PETER NORMAN

Mansfield Press

Copyright © Peter Norman 2010
All Rights Reserved
Printed in Canada

Library and Archives Canada Cataloguing in Publication

Norman, Peter, 1973-
      At the gates of the theme park / Peter Norman. -- 1st ed.

Poems.
ISBN 978-1-894469-46-3

      I. Title.

PS8627.O76A87 2010   C811'.6   C2010-901314-X

Editor for the Press: Stuart Ross
Design: Denis De Klerck
Typesetting: Stuart Ross
Cover Photo: iStockphoto
Author Photo: Steve Arthur

The publication of *At the Gates of the Theme Park* has been generously supported by
the Canada Council for the Arts and the Ontario Arts Council.

ONTARIO ARTS COUNCIL
CONSEIL DES ARTS DE L'ONTARIO

Canada Council   Conseil des Arts
for the Arts   du Canada

Mansfield Press Inc.
25 Mansfield Avenue, Toronto, Ontario, Canada M6J 2A9
Publisher: Denis De Klerck
www.mansfieldpress.net

for Melanie

CONTENTS

THREE-TONE ELECTRONIC FANFARE

Attention, shoppers:
in five minutes we will close.
The automatic sliding doors will lock
without warning and beyond our control.
Please bring your items to the front
for purchase now. Your hours of browsing—
stroking cans of soup with slender hands,
bending to examine avocados,
kissing parched sheaves of spaghetti—
are over. Proceed to the front.
Your baskets weigh you down,
bulbous with milk and pomegranate.
There is no point in continuing now.
We open at eight tomorrow: then
you may resume the spree
and come back with double the yearning
or triple—we don't mind. Tomorrow
is another shift, another crew.

Admit the essence of your need.
It is to hold the not yet consumed,
fondle its bumpy skin,
even to lay it in your basket
snug among cashews and corn.
It is not the register's blip
granting you dominion
with one brief syllable of assent;
not the drive home, acquisitions
colliding like dead wood in the trunk.
This is the apex of your longing: here,

regaled by our announcement,
rolling apples in a fevered palm,
craning to scope the undiscovered aisle:
here you are as glad,
as fed,
as ever.
Proceed to the front.

Dust, great cotton-candy wads of it.
Three paper clips.
Human hair: his own and yours,
intractably entwined.
Five cents in pennies.
Veins and arteries of thread,
bloodless, unpulsing in the dust.
Crumbs of a meal you shared
with him, that night
when hope stirred bravely
in the candlelight, in the sure flow
of wine from a neck unstopped.
Fingernail clippings.
A pencil's tip.
Charred wick and chips of cork.
Particles of sound: your chair
scraped back from the table;
voices, the mounting crescendo.
A busted thumbtack.
A spider asphyxiated.
Molecules and atoms, a ravelled mess,
a brood of dissonances made one.

SIGNS OF TROUBLE

An ambassador
of Jehovah's Kingdom
stutters on your porch,
asking you
for all the answers.

Three crows gather
on the wire that runs to your eaves.
When you look again
they are doves.

By the time you get to his house
he is smiling.
He wants to dance,
go somewhere wild.
On the phone, five minutes ago,
he was wretched with tears.

The milkman leaves
eleven bottles.
Normally it's twelve.

Next day the missing one
arrives. The fluid inside
is crimson.

Low batteries in your Walkman.
The favoured song
slows to a moan.

At last the words make sense.

NOCTURNE

I am on the porch with binoculars
in a column of moonlight
palpable as rain.

Below me, by a garden
fenced in against deer,
the dog whimpers in sleep.

Yards away
the woods flash predatory eyes.

Wind grips the tops of trees,
compels them to bend, forces
moans of protest
that swell and subside.

On its bucking branch an owl
spies a mole's head broken
through the surface of the soil,
and dives.

There are creatures nearby
that eat only plants.
There are creatures that lay their eggs
by the hundred.

There are things I've said that I regret,
even here, in this home, to you,
and there are currents of air
that turn and bend back
over themselves
impossibly.

The faint smell of something's death
passes over the bungalow,
spreads itself
to nothing.

I clamp the binoculars tight
to my face. I scan
the moon's plaintive eyes
for welling.

NESTING DOLL

A meaningless toy, it brought nightmares
that sent her shrieking into wakefulness,
summoning us or crying, simply, "Smaller!"
We'd flick off the TV and sprint upstairs
and find her shaking in her thin nightdress
soaked through with perspiration, stained with pee
or worse; and she would sob and shake and holler,
bury her face in stalwart teddy bears,
seek comfort from a toy in toys. I guess
we should have figured out the source. A father's
job, knowing his child. I ought to be
clairvoyant of the germ causing it all,
the thing my daughter dreaded she might see:
the shape inside the doll inside the doll.

PLUCKED

That afternoon, Miss Johnson taught us *S*,
how to shape its swollen belly.
My curves were wrong, deflated,
nothing like her samples on the board:
buoyant loops and curls
afloat in slate.

And I was plucked from class
early, leaving letters
half-made.

At home I had to pee.
"Don't look in the bath," Dad said, so I did,
peeled back the shower curtain,
wet skin of a secret.

I did not understand the towels,
limp, drooling dark fluid
on porcelain.
I drew the curtain closed.
On the toilet's cold rim I trembled,
releasing nothing.

Class, I guess, continued without me.
Letters were copied from the board.
A bell rang. Miss Johnson turned,
wielding a chamois,
and the chalk was smudged away.

STILL LIFE WITH ACTION

Tangerines roll to the table's edge.
Poltergeist-flung, a pomegranate
flattens its flesh against the wall.

All the blooms turn heliotrope,
bowing nebbish heads
as daylight hightails west.

Done bearing their beauty, the vase
dumps them with gusto but
tilts too far,
clatters to the floor and breaks.

Announcing it has legs, the table
jostles its load with a jig.
Air heaves itself into gale,
scattering cut stems.

The burden of a world
outside its frame defeats
the skylight. It implodes.

A sudden rainfall of glass
and grime and car exhaust,
commerce, fear, human sweat,
grand deluge of lust and swill.

I've got life lined up in my scopes,
but the damn thing won't keep still.

Don't be frightened by the oyster shells.
Their teeth are false, shaved
sharp. Those aren't real fangs.
The opening and closing is a trick
achieved with a small motor
activated by you, your weight, pressing
on the floor, right here. And don't be afraid
of the pearl. It isn't real. It isn't really melting.
It doesn't really ooze or spurt.

Please be calm. Don't let the dogs
make you nervous. In fact, they're not dogs.
They are animatronic beings. Their lack
of teeth startles only
the uninitiated. You'll get used
to the smack of revulsion, the pang
of nausea when the hinged jaw swings,
exposing mother-of-pearl gums
and a tongue shiny and slow
as a shucked mollusc.

I implore you: don't fear me.
These are not really pearls
that were my eyes. They're only glass
tarted up. Fake jewels, nothing weird.
Think of them, if it helps, as marbles.
Think of them as rubber balls
you can fling and bounce with tremendous force

off gym walls. Think of them as something
sweet. Wads of gum chewed white.
Pretend I don't repel you
and the skin you glimpse just under my skin
is normal, something people have,
and the hand spreading within my hand
has no desire to clutch you.

Think what you need to think
to feel safe.

RECURSION

I fall awake alone. Outside,
nocturnal rain ascends.

Alarms rage, summoning a thief
who hurries to the store,
unpacks his duffel sack,
replaces items on the shelf.

Morning. The plane dispenses you.
We enfold each other,
celebrating your undeparture.
Tears scroll up our cheeks,
nestle into ducts.

Last night we wake
sweat-soaked and sated,
breathe flame to candlewick
and fuse, hips coaxing sheets
to smoothness.

Years ago, our meeting is unmade.
My life hurries back into ignorance,
days spent unrolling snowballs,
being chased by the ice cream truck,
gathering bread spat by ducks
beside a cool lake.

We will never disentangle
at the baggage check.
You won't be tugged from me
by announcements,
gates, corridors, customs.

I am three years old.
I urge spilled milk into a jug,
right it on the table.
My mother's alarmed eyes
flash calm.

Outside, a robin
cocks her head,
feeds worms
to the hungry soil.

OVAL BAY

The bay is oval. At its head
the land forms pincers like a crab's.

A skiff is passing between the claws.
It carries everyone you love.

There aren't too many of them, so they fit
inside the hull. Haze gathers at the edge

of Oval Bay. The ship might disappear
but doesn't: fog is parted by its hull.

Fog-breaker. Useful on dim days
or bright ones when the fog's invisible.

And so you see the bifurcated fog
and at its cleft the stern of the loaded skiff.

What will you do? It's too far now to swim.
You should have done that sooner, if it helps

to swim after a boat powered by wind,
which motor is far bigger than a man

and omnipresent too.
And you're a man.

What will you do? The telephone won't work
because you dropped it in the sand. Its ring

crackles with the interfering grains. A noise
like barnacles crunched underfoot. What can you do?

There's nothing here suggesting deities
will hear you if you pray. Nothing at all

but rockscape studded with a clutch of trees
bent double by the gales. It's time

to make your mind up, sir. The stern
of the boat has gone so far, you can't make out
the fading words that would have made its name.

WITH YOUR CAMERA

You captured on film a reptile
luxuriating in its patch
of sun: blood
warming to a tepid peak
still nowhere near what we would know
as norm, we mammal types,
lactescent,
hot,

churning with sperm or estrogen,
with strands of protein spelling out
each need,
mucus to ease our breath,
wax and tears
to slide us through the arid years,
seminal fluids for conquering death.

*

I watched your film
of milk that spilled
and spread on a wooden floor.
Blurry in the background I could see
the man with ruptured shoulders
bang his fist on the kitchen door.

*

We were kids. You showed me
time-lapse footage of decay.

We started with an egg.
Proceeded to a tray of fruit.
Grew into birds and mice.

Culminated with an elephant.
The pulsing hide.
Tornado made of flies
rising to blacken the air
as on the day Christ died.

✻

Whales exist for a reason, you say,
showing no film.
Plus those fish
that prey below
belowest realms.

In crevasses
of subsea trench
swim things
no camera has seen.

Jaws too wide
for eyes to apprehend.
Function as form:
animals all teeth.
Bellies trail, forlorn balloons.

✻

So you captured on film a reptile.
With a lazy flick
of its tail it started to move.
Lumbered to the camera, belly bulk
swaying with each step,
gut scrotum-like.
And its elemental jaw
with teeth in receding rows
gaped wide as the lens could conceive,
swallowed the camera,
you, the screen, your audience.

And we were born and raised inside that gut.
Still the shadow play upon the stomach wall
does not convince. We know
there is a throat to clamber up,
a gate that opens and swings shut
according to reptilian whims,
a gate to let us out
into the breathing world,
the malls and cul-de-sacs,
the music roused by the bobbing baton,
the watchful guard outside the crematorium
and all the prayers and candles Earth contains;
the falcon wheeling with its ragged wing,
the chip that calculates the odds of anything
that might or will or has.

＊

The lizard yawns
and chomps into its prey.

Crunching tibiae
resound all down the throat.

AWAKE

That summer nightly she dreamed of machines
divorced from function. Trains in brambles, derailed.
Schooners caught on crags; rotting sails
the colour of gangrene.

In the neighbour's yard was an abandoned car,
hood up, motor pillaged, oil staining
yellow grass. Nights she heard it draining,
the gurgle of a flea drowned in a samovar.

In the dim moments at sleep's cusp
she'd enter the engine, explore its tanks
and tubing, sidle past the ranks
of pistons. She was intimate with rust

and uselessness, the grief of motion lost
and irreplaceable. As for her, she got worse.
The day came she required a full-time nurse,
a steep but necessary cost.

Outside, a rare wind outmoans the oil's seeping
and agitates the grass. She rises from her bed
and finds the door and slips onto the porch. Ahead,
the car shudders on its blocks. She can't be sleeping:

her toes touch dirt more solid than a dream's.
She slides behind the wheel. The doors close
gently with a click. The dashboard glows
and the hood is down; inside, the engine thrums.

Slip into gear. Lurch forward. The neighbour rushes
yelling from his house as his old Trans Am
lifts off. The town recedes. She slams
the accelerator, roars into fifth and flashes

at meteor speed through dusk.
Below, tide surges, lifting a boat
from its clutch of rocks. A train streaks out
from under brambles, grips the rail and thrusts

its carapace down a path set by engineers.
It reaches a tunnel.
It screeches, smoke belching from the funnel,
but cannot stop in time, and disappears.

A MAN ON THE BUS

A man on the bus
converses with himself.

Fierce rebuke in falsetto.
Cringing reply
in low, pleading tones.

Passengers look trapped
in the act of not looking.
The driver drives.

His foot is on the gas.
His badge is on his uniform.
His hand is ready on the horn.

But nothing cuts in front of him.
The horn will never sound.
We inch, as ever, from stop to stop.

LET ME KNOW

Please, dear, divulge in advance which bar
or eatery we will be going to.
I'll dress appropriate. I'll put on clothes
that make me seem the person such a place
would regularly serve. Looking up
from slathered wings or nachos or a plate
adorned with something tiny and gourmet,
patrons who see me when I saunter in, who spy
the shyness of my shyly sauntering in
and choose to comment will not say,
"Who's he?"

Instead they'll say, "Oh, him."

WINTER MORNING

Today the pane frost
is a map
of a lung
the coroner exhumed
from a cold chest.

I can see through it
to the year's first snow:
hefty flakes
hesitate
in their descent,
ride anxious whims
up, over, around.

Across the street
from our house
a woman falls.

A man holds out
his hand to her,
offering assistance
or asking for change.

I think her wrist is broken.
I think a link of spine is lost.

Her breath is an agitation around her.
The man's breath mingles with hers.
His hand is wrapped
in black wool,
a bandage or
a fingerless glove.

I can't hear his words
but I can see the air
that holds them.

Another woman,
out walking her dog,
unhooks it from its leash.

Its tongue steams
as it sprints
for the woman on the ground.

My chest is cold.
We didn't set the heat last night.
The snap was unexpected.

I lift a sweater
from a steel trunk
plastered with destinations.

After a moment's
wrestling with wool
my head and hands
emerge.

The women
and the man,
the dog and its tongue,
are gone.
Their footprints are meshed
and filling.

Something slips
from the folds of the sweater,
clinks on the floorboards.

I should bend
to pick it up.
I should put it
in a box
or on a high shelf,
out of the way.

But I won't do that.
I can't look at it.
I think I know
what it is,
though I can't be sure.

Filtered through
the simulacrum
of lung,
winter casts
a glow like that
of the adjustable lamp
in an autopsy room.

I think I can see
a shift
in the map,
a trickle
or twitch
in its compass of fronds.

AFTER THE DISASTER

We were kept
in a gym.
Lines on the floor
marked courts.

Mostly we slept.
A news crew came in
for a whirlwind tour
that was aired between weather and sports.

A fellow nearby
lost a mansion, he said.
God was to blame. It was theft.

I felt for the guy.
Then one day he rolled up his bed
and left.

UNWELCOME

Underfoot the cross-hatch
of needles shed and gone dark.
Crows patrol
the balding canopy.

I am not welcome on this turf.
The birds cluster,
roll shoulders at me.
A last wink, and the fire's out.

I came here to prove something
to myself, I seem to recall.
As if there's proof of anything
in huddling helpless.

As if reducing anything
to its base ingredient
would make it disappear
or change.

At my back, the rock face
helps the sun punch out.
We all labour in shifts
and some are shorter than others.

I hear the slinking of small things.
They are going about their business.
The cliff's shoulder is cold with moss.
I don't remember where I was before this.

SENTENCES

In the orchard
all the trees
wore bandages.

The bandages were broad
and overlapped,
glazed with resin
for catching caterpillars.

Flies and bees and ants
had landed and been trapped.

I picked an ant's wing
and its thorax twitched.

The bandages met my eyes
dead level.

I was five.

＊

Today I found
I could not lift
a bucket of green apples.

My breath was short.

Leaning on bark, I panted
at shorn turf
and regimented shrubs.

This is not the orchard
of my boyhood.

It's a trimmed yard.

Hired men edge
its lawns.

Last week the ants
were dispatched by a man,
freckled, a kid really,
with a cap and a dripping
nozzle for his poison.

His back was straight
as he administered it,
legs trunk-sturdy.

＊

Under the bandages
grew living wood.

Nothing was wounded; nothing
had been cut off.

Roots dived under soil,
rose again like leaping fish,
dived back.

But a bee twisted
trying to free itself
from the bandage, and instead
mired its one intact wing.

After that
it finally resigned.

*

I was surprised by this shortness
of breath, this failure
to lift a measly bucket.

I will have to take it slower
in the garden, now.

Manoeuvring to my knees
I will be ginger.

Once already I retired
after years of service
to a vocation.

Time was heavy then on my skull,
as on a humid day without wind,
and at last I was free to ask myself
how I had come to do
the kind of work I'd done.

There is a shed
at the end of this yard
decked with racks

hung with hoes
and rakes and claws
for turning earth.

How did I acquire these?

I would excise
all the judgments
lined up behind me
like cemetery markers
just cut, draped
with protective black tarp:
I would do this
without delay
or deliberation.

But they are stuck there
in the past
and won't be plucked.

＊

I did not stray far
into the orchard.

Stayed at the perimeter.

Dreaded the trunks' edging
toward me, convergence of white
bandages dotted with wings,
the jottings of an austere judge
dead level with my eyes.

PILOT

I carve
my autograph in earth. It's too bad
for those down there. Almost sad.
Who aren't blown up will starve
or go mad with grief. You serve
the enemy, you gag on the enemy's feast.
Some guys loop back, drop extra. It's a waste.
I stick to the flight plan, play it safe.

Once, on a low pass, I could see detail.
That's a day I'd rather blot out.
A building spilled children like shelled peas;
my payload threw them to their knees—
the siren had come too late.
I turned back to base to refuel.

BOY GERMS

Recess, and the Grade 5 kids
begin a round of kiss tag.
Boys gallop, arms outstretched,
clutching and touching with unaccustomed lips;
girls duck, dart away.

"Boy germs!" shrieks a girl and tags another,
and down the line the germs are passed
like gossip.

That age I swatted boy germs from my clothes,
unbraided and mussed my hair to shake them free;
I passed them on, declared immunity.

Today I wash and wash my hands.
I scour the floor
to scrape away whatever you have left.

But germs cleave:
pillowcases, sills, the hems of rugs:
my margins have been colonized for good.

On plates, under a scope, your fingerprint
squirms in every ridge.

THE SLOUGH

Man-dug ditch
lining the route to school
and back; paralysis of sludge
scum-caked, gelling; sibilant
haunt for flies and buzzing kin.

I was sent to Mac's for cottage cheese. Coming home along
the slough,
I got cornered by two boys and socked in the stomach.

It didn't hurt, but I dropped the cottage cheese
and some of it spilled, splashed over gravel.

As they watched, I got to my knees and gathered it up,
scraped it back into its plastic tub.

Root and vine choke the sloping
banks; sometimes a shopping cart
or fridge that didn't make it
down, snagged by wheel or wire,
dangles at the brink.

Outside the residential zone I biked past farms
with their dogs on long chains.

A truck went by, too close. Its back-breath toppled me.
I tumbled, bike and all, down the bank.

Rolling on stubble, I was able to grab a root. It held me
inches
from the muck. My bike was okay too, hooked at the chain
by a shrub.

In places the surface
breaks: upthrust, a spare tire's
algaed skin or trike wheel
greets the air. People throw
just about anything in there.

Stanley, my asthmatic classmate, has an older sister.
Retarded isn't quite the word. *She's not all there*, he says.

She's having sex with many of the boys her age.
She can't, or won't, refuse.

Word got out, of course, and now
the high school boys are knocking too.

Made for drainage, the slough
oozes discharge to the Fraser.
Stations placed at junctures measure
level, composition: how deep this is,
what it's made of.

Biking home I see her, Stanley's sister,
in some trees beside the slough.

A boy holds a knife to her throat. I know his long red hair.
Rumour has it he's her first and her most frequent.

Her eyes are held by his. For now I'm safe. Slinking away,
    I hear
his threat: "Everyone's talking. Shut your fucking mouth."

At summer's peak I dream I'm shoved
the whole way down, to the congealed scum.
I seem invisible, all blotted out
by swarming dots. They're flies, I think.
Then the skin splits, and I begin to sink.

RECURSION: THE OUTTAKE REEL

Fire engines back away from flame.
The building staggers to its feet,
reclaiming form.
Belongings are acquired,
and a home.

Magazines taunt you
with photos of merchandise
you should never have brought to the store.

Snakes from time to time encounter
husks of themselves.
They wriggle in
and slither on,
thicker but
lustreless.

Heat flows always
to the warmer body.
Nature strains toward order.

One by one my sins
are gathered up and tucked away,
forgotten but
not forgiven.

Adam slinks into Eden,
shedding his furs.
Prowls about stealing names.
Eats Eve.

Fire creates but
leaves us cold.

Let there be darkness.

My sister had toy squirrels,
the Woodsies—ma, pa, kid.
Squeeze 'em and they squeaked.

After a year or two the voices
ran dry. Stitches loosened.
Plastic feet snapped and tails
sloughed off, becoming wisps

of wool again. The Woodsies
smiled through it all until
the threads of their mouths came free.

This one, though, on the concrete,
this real one, is not naive.
It knows what's coming. Its fight
to live is just a chore.

Somehow a back leg broke
or came disjointed
and splays at eighty degrees.

Scrabbling, the squirrel
achieves a fitful orbit
of that bad leg.
Lungs shudder under fur.

If I were not a coward I would kill it
myself. Find a rock. Instead
I watch it drag its heft in circles.

We are alone in a parking lot
at the wooded base of Parliament
Hill. It's after five; no cars.
The civil servants are at home

where windows fill with television light
as if the deepest ocean fish,
bioluminescent with ludicrous jaws

and see-through scales,
skulked in tanks in Kanata
living rooms, house after house,
waiting for the bulbs to fail.

A breeze. Dry leaves shiver but won't
lift off. Trees flex to confer.
Something makes commotion in the woods,

ransacks the Hill for a lost morsel,
a nest filled with nuts or a coin
someone dropped on the way to the car,
flawless and shiny, hopelessly round.

THREE METAPHORS IN SEARCH OF ANTECEDENTS

_____ is a rancid avocado,
splendid with wrecked promise:
a decrepitude of soft green flesh
lost in a caved-in hide.

Who has time for _____ ,
the crevassed scrotum of its underside?

Avert your eyes from _____ .
It is a leprous dancer
waving his bandage-ends
for loose change
at the public market.
Shoppers drop their baskets and scream.
This is bad for business.
This kills whole economies.
Best advice is force your eyes
to look at something else.

IF I AM SUMMONED

I will be there in no time flat.
I will be there yesterday.
I will wait at the maternity ward
in a gown and surgical mask
for your debut request.

You're so demanding.
Not even born and it's
do this do
that.

I will be there if I am summoned
to monitor the protozoans that became
amoebas and fish and apes and us.

I will be there at the intake of breath
that preceded the Big Bang.
Make sure everything flings out okay.

Always one thing or the next.
Don't you know I have a life?
Dragging me out of bed
before the dawn of time.

THE SUN

after Stuart Ross after Georg Trakl

Something like soup is drooled from high clouds.
Ears flick to attention: a ray sneaks past.
Here is an overturned bug. Here is a syringe filled with sugar.

An oar shatters everything.
Put your hand to the fissure and feel the steam.
Management assumes no responsibility.

Insidious? Yes, but crucial too.
Sometimes it spits hail, sometimes a choir of angels.
I'm sorry about what happened. Really, I am. The curve of your
    neck is so beautiful.

OUR CITY, METICULOUS

Little trucks on treads nibble, incessant
as last April's ants,
at our sidewalks, every season,

shouldering snow aside or sweeping
litter, dead leaves, mowers' cud.

At dusk one autumn, pinned
by oncoming lights, I thought at last
the bristles had me singled for disposal.

Surely each pedestrian's dusk
will come, the advancing whisk or plow;

behind a screen of mesh the city prole
hits the gas, extrudes the mandibles,
bears down on the one outstanding flaw.

TORPOR

Insects, I learn, don't sleep.

Instead the system slows to near-
null, glides below the twitch
and tic of waking life,

something like trance,
a state of shock
or disbelief.

It's autumn, I'm ten,
and night presses in.
Wires buzz over the slough.

At the fringe of a copse
I kneel at a fern,
prod fronds, lift—

But nothing's there.
I thought I'd find them,
drowse-bound, cocooned

in semi-sleep. I thought I'd call
or pluck them into light,
each of them, by name.

ROUGH MONTH

Cry of a leaf detaching
at the stem from a twig: this cry
saturated the air all October
until the dirt was littered with spent cries.

The thing that happened that was planned
in the building, with the people. And the thing
that wasn't planned at all—same place,
same people, more or less.

People in attendance at the planned event
in their best dark clothes, and at the other,
the unplanned one, in their best dark clothes.
I don't think any of us change.

Treading on the bright bodies of leaves
we hurried inside, away from all the falling,
but then observed in the skin of a gourd
eyes and a mouth made by knife—

signal of the day we change
into new things, the day
we reach at last for the wall-hung calendar
and flip the page.

UNCLE, ENOUGH!

Greatcoat soaked with trouble,
Uncle tramps through the door.
Trouble shoulders in from the harbour in coils,
hauling cries from the big horn mounted
below the avid lighthouse eye.

Uncle has a long pine staff
knobbed at the top with a natural knot
where in its growing the pine struck doubt
and turned away, and back again, and stalled
in an eddy of its expected growth.

For decades we've listened to Uncle!
His tales, when he seeps them, ooze with fog
and sea growth, saddening whom they swallow.
For years all we've wanted is a day in a yard
bared to the onslaught of sun! A swing set! A pool!

For a pool of plastic moulded as a hippo
in whose plastic depression we could wallow,
we'd snap into kindling that old pine staff,
earn bucks from paunchy tourists when we strolled
without apparent pain on the path of its embers.

NO YOKEL

I'm no yokel.
Prove me wrong.
Generations have trod on my forefathers' throats,
and sometimes, yes, we've had to deal in goats,
but that was not our fault.
I was born in a modern hospital
and gleaming forceps yanked me free.
The doctors had all the technology.
You should have seen the sheen upon those rooms!
You should have seen the robot nurse
shiny as a new hearse
with her tinted eyes.
Look at my sophisticated mien.
My soft, pink hands are always clean.
The straw hat's just a prop.
I've lived in seven cities.

HIRED HELP

At Babel the janitor flung down his mop
and cursed in many tongues. In Babylon
the gardener planted omnivorous weeds.
The guy who polishes the big brass toes
at the base of the Colossus of Rhodes
stuck dynamite plugs in the backs of the knees.

A mob advances armed with brooms
debristled and beheaded. Sticks, I guess.
They are the sweepers of Versailles.
The swabbers of the stations of the cross.
Their limbs have been replaced with metal rods
and coins are watching me instead of eyes.

WINTER MORNING: THE NEXT MORNING

I found out what it was
I had dropped:

a precise metal ball,
part of an old bicycle
that had come apart in my hands.

＊

No, sorry, that's another time.
I was thinking of another time.
This time it was a penny
dated 1965.
The Queen looked young.

I'm sorry to waste your time with these details.
I am so serious about details.
I ought to lighten up.

＊

Okay, no, I admit:
I don't know what fell to the floor.
Maybe that maddens you.
Sure as hell bugs me.

Not to worry.
The point is, it was cold.
The point is, the frost.

Did you see it twitch?
There—

EXPLORER

Tramping through the Amazon in waders
up to your navel, you spied
a species of snake that tempts
entirely through telepathy.

He spurred you to taste
the flesh of a fruit
you'd never seen before
in any supermarket, nor the trails
of all the world's tropics, which you've scoured.

He promised boundless knowledge.
Promised singularity
of purpose and of soul.
Promised severance
from all that was past.
Truly *living in the moment.*

Which promise did he break?
He promised he'd break only one.

✳

Remember we stepped off the plane in Tepic
and gasped at the poultice of heat.

I at least gasped.
You were aloof
and had done it all before.
Let's find ourselves some whores.
Just moments off the plane!

I thought that I might suffocate
from the fetid air alone.
Human warmth would only make it worse.

But the whores, when we found them,
were cool to the touch. Eyes
congealed and aimed toward the walls.
Payment accepted with murmurs.

On the insect screen the moulted exoskeletons.
Spectres of anatomy
lifelike down to the leg,
the compound eye.

＊

Spelunking caverns measureless to man

＊

Shipwreck!
Gashed hull!
Treasures maybe in the sand-sunk chest!
Fish flit among the desiccated ribs!
A school of undulating gills!
A host of twitchy fins!
Footprints of Jesus visible above!
A scuba team with bendy, elongated feet!
A naval fleet!
The motes of silt!
The rangy squid!
Its watchful eye!

It's quiet here and bodies travel slow.
That's all we know. It's all we need to know.

*

We both gasped
(even blasé you)
when the fossil you pulled
from its display drawer
and placed on the table
for me to ogle
writhed.

THE FALL

What happened was, I fell off a horse
for the first time. Not just fell:
got scraped off by a branch
of pine I rode through but forgot to duck.

Others were with me, and their voices
gathered around that heap of me
slumped on peat imprinted by hooves.
And what they said was good and grand:

They said a corner had been turned.
Never a cowboy till you've fallen once.
Be brave. Dust off. I rose, and stepped
from dark, hard peat onto a floor of glass.

CONFESSION

I became for a while obsessed with seeds.
I collected them from the cruces of plants.
I scraped them from the undersides of leaves
and felt them cleave to my sweating hands.

I haven't told you about this phase.
It passed in secrecy.
Seems to me now as a disease
that smouldered, flared and died away.

But sometimes at night I rise
and sidle from our home.
I slink into the greenhouse,
its pollinated gloom.

I thrust my fingers into dirt
and burrow uselessly,
knowing full well the thing I want
will shrink away from me.

I was for a while obsessed with seeds.
Today they rarely cross my mind.
But somehow, now, I felt the need
to make confession, though I haven't sinned.

If one night you wake to find the bed
cooler, its other half unmanned,
don't worry. I'll come back; I always did.
Ignore the dirt that's clinging to my hand.

LITTLE REJECTION SLIPS

I have been opening your mail.
One in five or six submissions
is addressed to you.
I read on your behalf.
People thank you
for gentle rejection.

A man sent a play.
He's grateful for your note last time.
Hopes for another.
Says he has to live on those.

    I have read and read again
    your letter. Held it to the light
    in case you'd watermarked a change of mind.

The note was written in pen.
Felt. Blue.
I dare not write him back:
"She's gone.

You'll have to learn to live on something else."

TO AN OLD FRIEND

In seventh grade the nun
frowned at the note you'd written
and set it alight.

Remember the shrieking alarms,
the onslaught of red trucks,
the axe wrenched from its glass case
mounted on the wall?

*

God (who you say isn't there;
myself, I'm never sure) made us
organs that grow engorged
at just the crucial instant.

How many decisions have hinged

*

Pool-hopping as teens we reached the whale tank
of the aquarium. You slid in
as I cowered at the edge and watched

your conversations with the orca,
your frolic amid dolphins and your tryst
with hammerheads. You touched

their teeth. You stroked
their bulging brows.

*

Field trip to the western shore
where scientists inspect the ocean life.

It's all here
in this tidal pool.

Anemones billowing
but shrinking from your touch.

Shy crabs with claws held out
to ward you off.

Contusions of the rock.
A sludgy film.

Your face dim on the surface.
Mine behind it.

The one spot where your finger goes
to meet its rippled self.

Gimbals to hold level the rod.
Hydraulic pumps from the throne of God.
Gadgets of all description stuck
in dis- and re-connect.
An electronic krummhorn set
at ten to blast the wax from out your ears.
A kudu dead inside its amniotic vat.
An Inquisition rack.
Binoculars: a navy-issued pair
designed for naval gazing.

Sad-sack cache,
lamentable array
banished from the realm of worth.
The words that parrots say
before they peck the eye
or storks' remarks
upon a stillbirth.

STUFFED

after Margaret Avison

Somebody stuffs the world in at my eyes.
It's pre-digested; I just let it break
the antiquated locks on the optic doors. My rice
is grey as corpse flesh and my whisky quakes
when riot cops march by. Electric air
creates a raised-hair halo. Desolate,
I shunt my toys from gate to gate and bear
the unseen force of all that freight
crammed through lenses at the break of morning,
bleak as the Yangtze and the leprous welts
that huddle on its flesh as a kind of warning.
Abstract, the characters reveal little else
than a sad, inconsequential blur.
There is no change, no listener.

JUDGMENT

I saw a girl begging for change.
I gave her change, for she was beautiful.
But nothing shifted: next day she was there
still beautiful and begging. And the eye
she cast was cold, its judgment terrible.

My boss returned the annual report.
I'd written it. He'd circled things in red
that needed fixing. So I fixed those things
and sent it back. He sent it back again.
A dozen circles blotted every word.

Three storks delivered babies to my door.
The babies made much noise and ate much food.
What can you do? What else would you have done?
I fed them food and bore the noise
and one by one they crawled to better homes.

ACKNOWLEDGMENTS

Versions of poems in this collection first appeared in *Bywords Quarterly Journal*, *Event*, *The Fiddlehead*, *Forget Magazine*, *Literary Review of Canada*, *Matrix*, *The New Formalist*, *Prairie Fire*, *Prism International* and the chapbook *After Stillness* (above/ground press, 2004). The writing of much of the manuscript was funded by the City of Ottawa Arts Funding Program and the Ontario Arts Council.

Numerous people deserve gratitude for contributing in some way to individual poems in this book; I hope they know who they are. Particular thanks to Stephen Brockwell for incisive feedback on many of the poems. I am very grateful to Denis De Klerck and Leigh Nash at Mansfield Press, and to Stuart Ross—this collection was his idea, and his keen editorial eye defined it. The enthusiasm and support of my family—Edward, Susan, Wendy and Mark Norman—has been a lifelong blessing. Above all, for more reasons than can be given here, immeasurable thanks to the brilliant and beloved Melanie Little.

Born and raised in Vancouver, where he completed a Creative Writing BFA at the University of British Columbia, Peter Norman has since lived in Ottawa, Calgary and Halifax. His poetry and fiction have appeared in several periodicals and anthologies, including *Jailbreaks: 99 Canadian Sonnets* and the 2008 and 2009 editions of *The Best Canadian Poetry*. His first novel, *Emberton*, is forthcoming in 2011 from Douglas & McIntyre.

BOOKS FROM MANSFIELD PRESS

POETRY

Leanne Averbach, *Fever*
Diana Fitzgerald Bryden, *Learning Russian*
Alice Burdick, *Flutter*
Margaret Christakos, *wipe.under.a.love*
Pino Coluccio, *First Comes Love*
Gary Michael Dault, *The Milk of Birds*
Pier Giorgio Di Cicco, *Early Works*
Christopher Doda, *Aesthetics Lesson*
Rishma Dunlop, *Metropolis*
Suzanne Hancock, *Another Name for Bridge*
Jason Heroux, *Emergency Hallelujah*
Carole Glasser Langille, *Late in a Slow Time*
Jeanette Lynes, *The Aging Cheerleader's Alphabet*
David W. McFadden, *Be Calm, Honey*
Lillian Nećakov, *The Bone Broker*
Peter Norman, *At the Gates of the Theme Park*
Catherine Owen & Joe Rosenblatt, with Karen Moe, *Dog*
Corrado Paina, *Souls in Plain Clothes*
Jim Smith, *Back Off, Assassin! New & Selected Poems*
Robert Earl Stewart, *Something Burned Along the Southern Border*
Steve Venright, *Floors of Enduring Beauty*
Brian Wickers, *Stations of the Lost*

FICTION

Marianne Apostolides, *The Lucky Child*
Kent Nussey, *A Love Supreme*
Tom Walmsley, *Dog Eat Rat*

NON-FICTION

Pier Giorgio Di Cicco, *Municipal Mind*
Amy Lavender Harris, *Imagining Toronto*